STUDY GUIDE

WHEN
I LAY
MY ISAAC
DOWN

STUDY GUIDE

WHEN
I LAY
MY ISAAC
DOWN

Unshakable Faith in

Unthinkable Circumstances

CAROL KENT

NAVPRESS
Discipleship Inside Out®

NAVPRESS

Discipleship Inside Out®

NavPress is the publishing ministry of The Navigators, an international Christian organization and leader in personal spiritual development. NavPress is committed to helping people grow spiritually and enjoy lives of meaning and hope through personal and group resources that are biblically rooted, culturally relevant, and highly practical.

**For a free catalog go to www.NavPress.com
or call 1.800.366.7788 in the United States or 1.800.839.4769 in Canada.**

© 2011, 2013 by Carol Kent
Study guide by Amber Van Schooneveld

ISBN-13: 978-1-61291-452-7

Cover design by Arvid Wallen

Some of the anecdotal illustrations in this book are true to life and are included with the permission of the persons involved. All other illustrations are composites of real situations, and any resemblance to people living or dead is coincidental.

Unless otherwise identified, all Scripture quotations in this publication are taken from the *Holy Bible, New International Version*® (NIV®). Copyright © 1973, 1978, 1984, 2011 by Biblica, Inc.® Used by permission of Zondervan. All rights reserved worldwide. www.zondervan.com. The "NIV" and "New International Version" are trademarks registered in the United States Patent and Trademark Office by Biblica, Inc.® Other versions used include THE MESSAGE (MSG). Copyright © 1993, 1994, 1995, 1996, 2000, 2001, 2002. Used by permission of NavPress Publishing Group.

Printed in the United States of America

1 2 3 4 5 6 7 8 9 / 18 17 16 15 14 13

CONTENTS

*I*NTRODUCTION: HOW TO USE THIS STUDY GUIDE

When God seems the most absent, He is the most present.

If you are reading this study guide, then most likely you are facing, have faced, or are close to someone who is facing unthinkable circumstances. Each person's "Isaac experience" may look different. Perhaps a loved one is facing a terminal disease, or your spouse is leaving you, or you are coping with a miscarriage or unemployment.

Whatever your Isaac experience is, you are faced with a choice. *What will you do in response?*

How do you survive each day? How do you simply "do the next thing"? But most of all, what will be your response to God? When unthinkable circumstances enter your life, there comes a point when you either stand by what you believe or walk away from it. Will you curl up in the alluring fetal position, or will you struggle on to find God, hope, purpose, and passion amid your circumstances?

This study guide will help you along in your journey of answering these questions — of struggling through the "whys" while still leaning into God as your comfort.

Each chapter of this study guide has two parts. The first is for individual reflection and journaling, for you to process through your thoughts, questions, prayers, and response. The second part is for you to go through with a small group who is either reading the book with you or watching the *When I Lay My Isaac Down* DVD together.

If you are reading the book together with a small group, complete the individual reflection section before each meeting. If you are watching the DVD together rather than reading the book, you can complete the individual reflection section after each meeting to go deeper.

You'll find extra lines in the group discussion section, where you can jot down ideas about specific things you would like to share with your small group, or you can use that space to take notes on helpful comments made by your group members.

If your group is large, you'll want to break into groups of about four to give everyone a chance to speak and feel comfortable being open.

Create an atmosphere of trust and safety within your group as you discuss these difficult questions. Agree not to discuss what other people have shared outside of the group, and commit to be "stretcher bearers" for one another, lifting one another up in prayer and support.

May God use this study guide to comfort you, challenge you, and bring you closer to Him. May He use it in your life to cement an unshakable faith even amid unthinkable circumstances.

chapter one

*A*N UNEXPECTED JOURNEY

The Power of Unthinkable Circumstances

There are moments when God makes utter and complete sense to us, and then suddenly, life changes and he seems a foreign remnant of a childhood force-fed faith. . . . "[Lord], give us eyes to see your coming and going, ears to hear your voice and your silence, hands to hold your presence and your absence, and faith to trust your unchanging nature in all seasons."

—ELISA MORGAN

ON *Y*OUR OWN: INDIVIDUAL REFLECTION

1. "Unthinkable circumstances" — circumstances that derail our carefully thought-out plans for our future — look different for each individual. In your own experience, current or past, what would you consider your "Isaac" experience?

_____

_____

_____

_____

_____

_____

_____

2. When tragedy strikes, we face a number of reactions: shock, paralysis, dizziness, anger. Carol found herself "sometimes angry, often hurt, always broken." What were some of your initial reactions to your situation? Which of those were constructive, and which were destructive?

CONSTRUCTIVE REACTIONS	DESTRUCTIVE REACTIONS

3. One of our first reactions when we face tragedy is to cry out to God, though often what we're feeling "words cannot express."

> In the same way, the Spirit helps us in our weakness. We do not know what we ought to pray for, but the Spirit himself intercedes for us through inward groans. (Romans 8:26)

Have you ever experienced this? How does it comfort you to know that the Spirit is with you, interceding on your behalf?

_____

_____

_____

_____

_____

4. Write here your current prayer to God. Maybe you're confused, angry, tired, or even hopeful. Maybe you need His comfort or strength. Or maybe you need the Spirit to intercede for you.

_____

_____

_____

_____

_____

_____

5. One of Satan's tricks is to whisper lies in our ears that go straight to our hearts and cause us to doubt God and truth. They might be that God doesn't love you or that you should have been a better Christian or even that as a good Christian you shouldn't have to suffer. What three lies are you tempted to listen to because of your circumstances?

Lie #1 _____

_____

_____

Lie #2 _____

_____

_____

Lie #3 _____

_____

_____

Summing it all up, friends, I'd say you'll do best by filling your minds and meditating on things true, noble, reputable, authentic, compelling, gracious — the best, not the worst; the beautiful, not the ugly; things to praise, not things to curse. (Philippians 4:8, MSG)

The lies Satan whispers into our ears are "the worst" and "the ugly." In Philippians, Paul told us to not fill our minds with the worst but to meditate "on things true." Replace the three lies you wrote with truth. What truth from the Bible or verse can you replace these lies with?

Truth #1 _____

_____

_____

_____

Truth #2 _____

_____

_____

_____

Truth #3 _____

_____

_____

_____

If you need some help finding truth to cling to in the Scripture, try starting with these verses: Isaiah 49:14-16 (God has not forgotten you); Jeremiah 31:3 (God loves us with an everlasting love.); Psalm 103:12 (God has removed our transgressions from us); Daniel 9:9 (God is merciful and forgiving); Psalm 34:18 (God is close to you when you are brokenhearted); 2 Corinthians 1:3-4 (God is your Comforter).

6. How can you actively choose to replace the lies you wrote with the truth of Scripture? Write here some practical and active ways you'll choose to meditate on the truth.

_____

_____

_____

_____

_____

7. Are you asking for help from other people? If not, what keeps you from asking? Embarrassment or self-reliance? Carefully consider what might help you right now: professional advice? A shoulder to cry on? Help with errands? Whom can you ask to help you with these needs?

_____

_____

_____

_____

_____

_____

_____

_____

8. The largest choice we have to make when facing unthinkable circumstances is to either stand by what we believe or walk away from God. After many of His disciples left Him, Jesus asked the Twelve, "'Do you also want to leave?' Peter replied, 'Master to whom would we go? You have the words of real life, eternal life'" (John 6:67-68, MSG). Where are you in this process? Have you firmly made up your mind to stay, or are you still unsure about God? Be honest with God about how you are feeling.

_____

_____

_____

_____

_____

_____

_____

_____

9. Discovering the power and the invaluable lessons found in unthinkable circumstances usually takes a great deal of time. If you can already articulate some of the things you've learned and ways you've grown, write them down as a

testament to God's faithfulness even amid devastation and sorrow. (If you have no idea what your circumstances are telling you, gently let yourself "off the hook" and accept that your experience is a process.)

_____

_____

_____

_____

_____

_____

_____

_____

_____

GROUP DISCUSSION QUESTIONS

Before launching into your discussion, turn to the person sitting next to you and answer this question in one or two sentences: *What is one thing on your mind that could distract you from hearing what God wants to say to you today?*

1. We each have faced our own unthinkable circumstances. Share with one another an "Isaac" experience from your past or one you are facing now. What were some of your reactions that were constructive and not so constructive? (Sharing stories can take a lot of time. Share about your experience briefly, giving everyone who wishes to share a chance.)

_____

_____

_____

_____

_____

_____

2. Read James 1:2-8 out loud together:

> Consider it pure joy, my brothers and sisters, whenever you face trials of many kinds, because you know that the testing of your faith produces perseverance. Let perseverance finish its work so that you may be mature and complete, not lacking anything. If any of you lacks wisdom, you should ask God, who gives generously to all without finding fault, and it will be given to you. But when you ask, you must believe and not doubt, because the one who doubts is like a wave of the sea, blown and tossed by the wind. That person should not expect to receive anything from the Lord. Such a person is double-minded and unstable in all they do.

How have your trials developed your perseverance, maturity, and wisdom?

_____

_____

_____

_____

3. Which of James' instructions are hard for you? What's hard about them?

_____

_____

_____

_____

4. It's completely normal in times of extreme trial for our prayers to be "wind-whipped." How would you describe your prayer life right now?

0	1	2	3	4	5
almost nonexistent		pretty windblown		clear, full of faith	

5. Satan tried to defeat Carol by making her believe lies, such as she was a bad parent or could have prevented the tragedy if she were a perfect Christian. What lies have you been tempted to believe in your situation?

_____

_____

_____

_____

_____

6. Is there a particular verse you cling to that is your life preserver of truth when you hear these lies?

_____

_____

_____

_____

7. Read Philippians 4:8 together:

> Summing it all up, friends, I'd say you'll do best by filling your minds and meditating on things true, noble, reputable, authentic, compelling, gracious — the best, not the worst; the beautiful, not the ugly; things to praise, not things to curse. (MSG)

What are some practical ways that you can actively fill up your mind with the truth of Scripture, replacing Satan's lies?

_____

_____

_____

_____

_____

8. Is your situation driving you toward God or away from Him? Have you decided to stick with Him, or do you still feel unsure about God and whether you can trust Him?

_____

_____

_____

_____

_____

9. In what way do you need support from others right now, and how can you pray for one another?

_____

_____

_____

_____

chapter two

*L*AYING ISAAC DOWN

The Power of Relinquishment

We can hug our hurts and make a shrine out of our sorrows or we can
offer them to God as a sacrifice of praise. The choice is ours.

—RICHARD EXLEY

ON *Y*OUR OWN: INDIVIDUAL REFLECTION

1. One of our first reactions to the Isaac experiences in our lives is to ask, and
sometimes shout, "Why?!" We are desperate for answers and direction from
God. Sometimes we receive answers and direction through Scripture or other
believers, but other times God might seem utterly silent. What has your
experience been? Do you feel that God has given you direction or answers, and
if so, what?

_____

_____

_____

_____

_____

_____

_____

2. Has God remained seemingly silent? If so, how has this affected you and your relationship with God? Has it forced you to trust in God's goodness and faithfulness, or has it caused you to question if He is even listening?

_____

_____

_____

_____

_____

3. Often our Isaac experiences leave us powerless to fix or change our situation — they are out of our control. How have you tried to control your situation in the past? By trying to force solutions? By controlling things outside of the situation, such as working too much or eating too little? By refusing to take "no" for an answer?

_____

_____

_____

_____

_____

_____

4. According to Carol, *relinquishment* means "giving up my rights to control the person, dream, expectation, or preferred outcome of the object of my concern." What are you trying to control — a person, a dream, or an expectation? What is your preferred outcome that you are trying to control?

The Object of My Control: _____

_____

_____

_____

_____

My Preferred Outcome: _____

_____

_____

_____

_____

5. Carol says, "When we release our grasp, our relinquishment puts a stop to our manipulation of other people and releases the Holy Spirit to do the supernatural through the power of prayer." Do you think your attempts to control your situation have gotten in the way of how God wants to work through the situation? How?

_____

_____

_____

_____

_____

6. Abraham was able to surrender his Isaac because he trusted in God's faithfulness, even without knowing there would be a positive outcome.

> We know that in all things God works for the good of those who love him, who have been called according to his purpose. (Romans 8:28)

Right now, do you believe this to be true — that God will somehow work good out of this situation, that He is trustworthy and faithful? Write your thoughts here.

_____

_____

_____

_____

_____

_____

7. Even when we submit our control to God and believe He will work out a situation for good, the outcome may not be what we desired.

> Though he slay me, yet will I hope in him. (Job 13:15)

> Shadrach, Meshach, and Abednego answered King Nebuchadnezzar, "Your threat means nothing to us. If you throw us in the fire, the God we serve can rescue us from your roaring furnace and anything else you might cook up, O king. But even if he doesn't, it wouldn't make a bit of difference, O king. We still wouldn't serve your gods or worship the gold statue you set up." (Daniel 3:16-18, MSG)

Even if the outcome is the opposite of what you desire, are you willing to still hope in God and worship Him? Do you echo the sentiments in Job and Daniel, or are you still struggling with the "yet will I hope in him"?

_____

_____

_____

_____

_____

_____

8. Have you or will you relinquish control of your situation to God, submitting to His will and trusting in His faithfulness? God won't force you to make the sacrifice. If you are ready, make this prayer your own:

> God, please help me through this time of suffering. I give up my right to control the outcome of _____
> [your Isaac experience]. I make this my heart sacrifice to You. I pray that Your Holy Spirit will continue to work in this situation and help me to continually relinquish this situation to You. God, I know that You love me more than I love _____
> [the object of your control], and I know I can trust You with the outcome. But though You "slay me" or _____

[the outcome you most fear], yet will I _____
[love God, serve Him, trust Him, worship Him].

9. True heart sacrifice involves embracing God's love in the process of release and resting in the outcome, even if we don't understand it. How can you practically take steps to embrace God's love and rest in the outcome? (Here are some ideas: reading some of God's promises each day, resubmitting your Isaac first thing each morning (and as often as necessary after that), confessing your love for God in prayer every day and accepting His love in return.)

_____
_____
_____
_____
_____
_____
_____
_____

10. The Christian life inherently involves losing our lives; we choose to allow ourselves to sink into darkness and be buried. Jesus said,

> Listen carefully: Unless a grain of wheat is buried in the ground, dead to the world, it is never any more than a grain of wheat. But if it is buried, it sprouts and reproduces itself many times over. (John 12:24, MSG)

Do you believe that God can use this seed and multiply it "many times over" to bless others or glorify Himself? How have you seen this already happening or how do you see God using this Isaac experience in the future?

_____
_____
_____
_____

_____
_____
_____
_____

11. Where are you in your process of relinquishment? Be honest with God and write out a prayer to Him about where you are right now and what you're struggling with.

_____
_____
_____
_____
_____
_____
_____
_____

GROUP DISCUSSION QUESTIONS

1. Get with one or two partners. In a sentence or two, tell your partners one thing you have been thinking about God this week or how last week's session has been challenging you.

_____
_____
_____
_____
_____
_____
_____

2. Read Genesis 22:1-18. If you were Abraham, what would have been going through your mind as you headed toward the mountain of sacrifice?

_____

_____

_____

_____

_____

_____

_____

3. What picture of God does this passage give you?

_____

_____

_____

_____

_____

_____

_____

4. What has been your personal "Isaac" — the cherished person, thing, desire, habit, dream, or position you've needed to relinquish in order for God to release His power?

_____

_____

_____

_____

_____

_____

_____

5. In your Isaac experience, have you tried to take control or fix the "problem"? What do you find yourself doing to control your situation? Busying yourself so you don't have to think about it? Bargaining with God? Eating, succumbing to depression, or getting mad?

_____

_____

_____

_____

_____

_____

_____

6. Read Genesis 16:1-4:

> Sarai, Abram's wife, had borne him no children. But she had an Egyptian slave named Hagar; so she said to Abram, "The LORD has kept me from having children. Go, sleep with my slave; perhaps I can build a family through her."
>
> Abram agreed to what Sarai said. So after Abram had been living in Canaan ten years, Sarai his wife took her Egyptian slave Hagar and gave her to her husband to be his wife. He slept with Hagar, and she conceived.
>
> When she knew she was pregnant, she began to despise her mistress.

Before the act of faith we see in Genesis 22, Abraham had doubted God and taken control of his situation. Whom can you relate to more right now — the Abraham of Genesis 16 or Genesis 22? Does it comfort you in your own situation to see how Abraham's faith had progressed?

_____

_____

_____

_____

_____

_____

_____

7. What would relinquishing your Isaac for five minutes involve? What about relinquishing your Isaac for a week?

_____

_____

_____

_____

_____

8. Read John 12:23-26:

> Jesus replied, "The hour has come for the Son of Man to be glorified. Very truly I tell you, unless a kernel of wheat falls to the ground and dies, it remains only a single seed. But if it dies, it produces many seeds. Anyone who loves their life will lose it, while anyone who hates their life in this world will keep it for eternal life. Whoever serves me must follow me; and where I am, my servant also will be. My Father will honor the one who serves me."

What would it mean for you to allow your "kernel of wheat" to fall to the ground and die?

_____

_____

_____

_____

_____

9. Why would God want us to relinquish what we love most? If you have had an experience like this in the past, describe how the kernel produced "many seeds."

_____

_____

_____

_____

_____

_____

_____

10. True heart sacrifices involve:

- Identifying something precious to you (your Isaac)
- Letting go of your control over the situation, event, or person as an act of worship
- Embracing God's love in the process of the release
- Resting in the outcome, even if in this lifetime you are not allowed to understand the reason behind the need for the sacrifice and the pain involved

If you're currently facing an Isaac experience, what part of this difficult process are you in?

_____

_____

_____

_____

_____

_____

_____

_____

11. How can the group pray for you today?

_____

_____

_____

_____

_____

_____

chapter three

*W*HY DIDN'T GOD *DO* SOMETHING?

The Power of Heartache

Heartache forces us to embrace God out of desperate, urgent need. God is never closer than when your heart is aching.

—JONI EARECKSON TADA

ON *Y*OUR OWN: INDIVIDUAL REFLECTION

1. How have you typically dealt with heartache in the past? For example, have you cried easily, or have you avoided crying? Do you find crying helpful, embarrassing, or both?

_____

_____

_____

_____

2. Reflect on why you do what you do with your sadness. Write your thoughts here.

_____

_____

_____

_____

_____

_____

3. Have you experienced the timely presence of a "comforting companion," who showed up for you in a powerful and unforgettable way when you most needed it? Write about it here, and then also write a note of thanks to this friend.

_____

_____

_____

_____

_____

4. Read 2 Corinthians 1:3-4:

> Praise be to the God and Father of our Lord Jesus Christ, the Father of compassion and the God of all comfort, who comforts us in all our troubles, so that we can comfort those in any trouble with the comfort we ourselves receive from God.

Recall a time when God used the brokenness of your heart to comfort someone else in a meaningful way, big or small. What different perspective did this experience give you about your own heartache?

_____

_____

_____

_____

_____

5. Think of someone you know who is currently experiencing heartache. How might you "show up" for this person as a comforting companion, even if it's from a distance? (Be creative!)

_____

_____

_____

_____

_____

_____

6. When was the last time you wondered, *Why didn't God do something?* Make a list of all the thoughts and emotions you experienced (or are now experiencing) while in the wilderness of *why?*

YOUR *WHY* QUESTIONS	THE THOUGHTS AND EMOTIONS OF THIS *WHY*

7. In John 11:35, it says that "Jesus wept" when He heard from Martha and Mary about Lazarus's death. How does it comfort you to know Jesus wept, most likely in response to the grief of His dear friends?

_____

_____

_____

_____

_____

8. Read Psalm 56:8: "You've kept track of my every toss and turn through the sleepless nights, each tear entered in your ledger, each ache written in your book" (MSG).

Think of the last time you spent a night tossing in bed. Next picture God there, watching and keeping track of each turn. Now think of the last time you cried. Picture God there, making note of every single tear. How do you respond to this incredible verse that God cares intimately about every ache and tear and sleepless night?

_____

_____

_____

_____

_____

9. Psalm 34:18 says, "The LORD is close to the brokenhearted and saves those who are crushed in spirit." How has heartache brought you closer to God? Have you experienced a time of close intimacy and dependence on God as a result of brokenheartedness?

_____

_____

_____

_____

_____

10. Psalm 91:1-2 says, "Whoever dwells in the shelter of the Most High will rest in the shadow of the Almighty. I will say of the LORD, 'He is my refuge and my fortress, my God, in whom I trust.'"

What would it mean for you to dwell in God's shelter or to rest in His shadow? How can you make Him your hiding place and fortress in times of heartache?

_____

_____

_____

_____

_____

11. Carol prayed, "Father, I am so broken, hurting, and totally unable to find peace. . . . I just want to quit living. I am weary of this pain that never goes away. Please rescue me. And if You do not remove me from this place of hurt, will You please climb inside this afghan with me and hold me? What do You want me to see? To learn? I am listening. Do You have anything to tell me?"

Consider writing here your own prayer to God. Allow God into the crushed places inside you and ask Him to embrace you with a comfort beyond anything you've experienced before. (If you're not experienced with this level of communication with God, give it time and repeat your heartfelt prayers often!)

_____

_____

_____

_____

_____

_____

_____

_____

_____

_____

GROUP DISCUSSION QUESTIONS

Because this is a particularly personal session, please remember your ground rule about not trying to fix people. Give people space to be angry or sad without having to make it all better.

1. Tell a partner one thing you have been thinking about God this week or one thing that has distracted you from Him.

_____

_____

_____

_____

_____

_____

_____

_____

_____

2. Read Psalm 13:

> How long, LORD ? Will you forget me forever?
>   How long will you hide your face from me?
> How long must I wrestle with my thoughts
>   and day after day have sorrow in my heart?
>   How long will my enemy triumph over me?
> Look on me and answer, LORD my God.
>   Give light to my eyes, or I will sleep in death,
> and my enemy will say, "I have overcome him,"
>   and my foes will rejoice when I fall.
> But I trust in your unfailing love;
>   my heart rejoices in your salvation.
> I will sing the Lord 's praise,
>   for he has been good to me.

Do you think it's a contradiction for this poet to ask, "How long?" but still claim that he trusts God? Have you ever been able to strike this balance yourself? Do you think it's okay to ask God questions like "How long?" and "Why?"

_____

_____

_____

_____

_____

_____

_____

3. Which of these emotions do you relate to most right now?

_____

_____

_____

_____

_____

_____

_____

4. How do you typically express these emotions? In tears? By hiding them to be "strong"?

_____

_____

_____

_____

_____

_____

_____

5. When was the last time you wondered, *Why didn't God do something?* What thoughts and emotions did you experience (or are you now experiencing) while in the wilderness of *Why?*

_____

_____

_____

_____

_____

_____

_____

6. Psalm 34:18 says, "The LORD is close to the brokenhearted and saves those who are crushed in spirit." How has God used brokenness or heartache in the past to draw you closer to Him?

_____

_____

_____

_____

_____

_____

_____

7. Read 2 Corinthians 1:3-4:

> Praise be to the God and Father of our Lord Jesus Christ, the Father of compassion and the God of all comfort, who comforts us in all our troubles, so that we can comfort those in any trouble with the comfort we ourselves receive from God.

This verse refers to God as "the Father of compassion and the God of all comfort." How does it make you feel to know that God is the Father — the

Creator — of comfort? Have you allowed God to be your Comforter, or in your hurt is it hard to be vulnerable with God like this?

_____

_____

_____

_____

_____

_____

8. When has God used the brokenness of your heart to enable you to minister to someone else in a meaningful way, big or small? How did that experience give you a different perspective of your own heartache?

_____

_____

_____

_____

_____

_____

9. How can the group pray for you today?

_____

_____

_____

_____

_____

chapter four

STRETCHER BEARERS AND YELLOW ROSES

The Power of Community

A friend hears the song in my heart and sings it to me when memory fails.

—ANONYMOUS

ON YOUR OWN: INDIVIDUAL REFLECTION

1. What kind of caring community have you experienced during a difficult time? Reflect on a time when others were able to carry your burdens for you.

_____

_____

_____

_____

_____

_____

_____

_____

_____

2. Is it hard for you to admit that you can't "make it" alone, or are you good at asking for help when you need it? Write here what your approach has generally been in the past when you've needed help.

_____

_____

_____

_____

_____

_____

3. Carol says, "I discovered what real 'community' is and how God designed people — through relatives and the friends in my life — to help me experience the unconditional love and compassion of Jesus."

Have your experiences of being cared for by others helped you better understand Christ's unconditional love for you? His compassion for you? Describe what you have learned about God's personal care for you through the actions of your own "stretcher bearers."

_____

_____

_____

_____

_____

_____

_____

4. Galatians 6:2 says, "Carry each other's burdens, and in this way you will fulfill the law of Christ." What do you think is meant by this statement?

_____

_____

_____

_____

_____

_____

_____

5. If you are in the middle of your own Isaac experience, who knows about it? How much do they know? How much do you keep private, and why?

_____

_____

_____

_____

_____

_____

_____

_____

_____

6. If your Isaac experience is in the category of heart sacrifices that involve difficult personal choices, your needs may not be immediately evident to those around you. What first step might you take to open the door to others who could help bear your burden?

_____

_____

_____

_____

_____

_____

_____

_____

7. Who are your personal "stretcher bearers"? Make a list of the people in your community of helpers and list some of the ways they have "been Jesus" to you. (Remember, even if you don't have a huge network, you can get through a tragedy with even just one person supporting you.)

My Helpers	How They've "Been Jesus" to Me

Say a prayer of thanks to God for each one of them, and consider how you can thank them for how they have helped you already.

_____

_____

_____

_____

_____

_____

8. Philippians 2:3-4 says, "Don't push your way to the front; don't sweet-talk your way to the top. Put yourself aside, and help others get ahead. Don't be obsessed with getting your own advantage. Forget yourselves long enough to lend a helping hand" (MSG).

At times in our lives, the best therapy is to "forget ourselves" and "lend a helping hand." Is there a time you helped others and it helped you to cope with your own personal struggles? How?

_____

_____

_____

_____

_____

_____

_____

_____

9. There are different ways we can be "stretcher bearers" for others: writing letters of encouragement, listening, providing for material needs, praying. In what way do you think God has specifically gifted you to be able to help others? Remember: "Help needy Christians; *be inventive* in hospitality" (Romans 12:13, MSG, emphasis added).

_____

_____

_____

_____

_____

_____

_____

_____

_____

_____

10. Is there someone in your sphere of influence who needs some kind of assistance or encouragement? List the needs of this individual or family and consider what you could do to help meet one or more of these needs. (And remember the creativity of the men who even "went through the roof" to help a friend.)

MY FRIENDS' NEEDS	HOW I COULD CARRY THEIR BURDENS

GROUP DISCUSSION QUESTIONS

1. With one or two partners, discuss one thing you have been thinking about God this week or one thing that has distracted you from Him.

_____

_____

_____

2. Read Luke 5:17-26. If you were the paralytic, what would you be feeling or thinking

- in verses 18-19?
- in verse 20?
- in verses 21-23?
- in verses 24-25?

3. What do you think this story says about Jesus — His identity, personality, and priorities?

_____

_____

_____

_____

_____

_____

_____

4. Are you more comfortable being on the giving end or the receiving end of active caring? Why?

_____

_____

_____

_____

_____

_____

_____

5. Is it hard for you to admit that you can't make it alone? When was the last time you did?

_____

_____

_____

_____

_____

_____

6. Tell about a time in the past when someone acted as your "stretcher bearer." Tell about how he or she was Jesus for you or helped carry you to Jesus.

_____

_____

_____

_____

_____

_____

7. Romans 12:13 says, "Help needy Christians; be inventive in hospitality" (MSG). What are some ways in which you can "be inventive" in helping others, like the paralytic's friends? What gifts has God given you to help others?

_____

_____

_____

_____

_____

_____

8. If you need "stretcher bearers" in your life right now, say so here and explain how and why.

_____

_____

_____

9. Is there anything you can do as a group for someone in or outside your group who has a need? *PRAYer 5mo. 2yRS*

_____

_____

_____

_____

_____

10. Because this session is about community, it's a great chance to assess how effective your group is as a community. Save time to discuss these two questions:

- What's going well in our group?
- What could we do better to be a powerful community for one another?

11. How can the group pray for you today?

_____

_____

_____

_____

_____

chapter five

*E*VEN IN THIS . . .

The Power of Hope

> *Our broken lives are not lost or useless. God's love is still working. He comes in and takes the calamity and uses it victoriously, working out his wonderful plan of love.*

—ERIC LIDDELL

ON *M*Y OWN: INDIVIDUAL REFLECTION

1. Think back on your life and ask God to bring to mind times when He has brought some kind of victory out of calamity. Write about them here. How do they give you hope?

Abuse - Parents became Christians
Drugs + Suicide - Dr. Charge* 2 (3x wk) for 2½ years.
Loss of Son - Turned me back to Jesus 3 wks he died
Suicide - with guns + He blinded me - Scream for Help.
Hospital gave me time to see Jesus in life again.
Accident - help to concord Depression - want to live.
Divorce - made me fight and stand with Jesus.
Son - Live see the work of the Lord + strengthens me.

Consider designating a small notebook or journal in which you will record past and future evidence of how God is salvaging your calamities for redemption.

2. What is an area or circumstance in which you are holding on to hope? What exactly are you hoping for?

*Scott - AA - work on * "accepting Jesus"*
*Tim - relys on self * accepting Jesus*

Craig - 65 days not just words but complete change of mind + soul

3. Has anything in this chapter altered your position or perspective in any way? Write down what has challenged or encouraged you and ask God to reveal more to you in the days ahead.

Letting Go of past - others have made it with same positions

4. Even if we don't get what we are hoping for in this lifetime, have you made the decision to still love, trust, obey, honor, and worship God, *even if nothing changes?* Even if there is no "happily ever after"? Does this idea scare you, give you hope, or seem too hard?

Yes Hope Jesus is my only Hope.

5. Read Psalm 62:5-7:

> Find rest, O my soul, in God alone;
>> my hope comes from him.
> He alone is my rock and my salvation;
>> he is my fortress, I will not be shaken.
> My salvation and my honor depend on God;
>> he is my mighty rock, my refuge.

Do you think the desired outcome of your situation has become your hope? Or are you truly clinging to God as your hope and refuge?

His will be done – No matter What – Help me to accept. Outcome!

Write out this passage on an index card and place it where you can read it often. Memorize it and then intentionally meditate on it every day for at least one week. At the end of that week, notice if anything about your attitude or position has changed.

6. Psalm 27:13-14 says,

> I remain confident of this:
>> I will see the goodness of the LORD
>> in the land of the living.
> Wait for the LORD;
>> be strong and take heart
>> and wait for the LORD.

Can you agree with the psalmist, saying, "I am still confident of this: I will see the goodness of the LORD in the land of the living"? If not, what is holding you back? What do you think this "goodness" consists of?

Yes - Jesus was with me when I Hide His word gave me strength even when I thought there was no hope. He Cared me.

7. Carol says, "Hope becomes unsinkable when we realize our hope is not in having spouses or friends who will never disappoint us, or in enjoying financial security, or in achieving a certain level of success, or in having perfect health, or in watching children turn out exactly as we had anticipated. Hope remains constant when we get to know the Source of all hope."

If hope truly does lie only in knowing the Source of hope, what specific steps can you take toward knowing this Source better — toward making Him your rock, salvation, fortress, and refuge?

Spend time with Him in prayer - word - attitude of mind.

8. We can't always know how God will redeem a situation for good. In this lifetime, we may never know all the ways in which God can extract something of value out of horrendous circumstances. Think through your own circumstances, and write down the ways in which you think God has been or might be working to redeem them for His own glory.

Brother helping Brother

Son's call – not to judge Jay but to be careful of him.

9. Whom do you know, personally or by reputation, whose experience of redemption in the midst of devastation inspires you? How do his or her stories encourage and strengthen you?

Brian Spencer – Gay but was a missionary to China – when single infatuated with him. Then he told me his problem. Never wanting to give in – but work for the Lord. Prayed death before weeking – died 4 years later to cancer. Was happy even in death.

Write a note of thanks for this person's role as a hope-giver and, if possible, send it to him or her.

10. Henry Blackaby stated, "Every Christian is called by God to be on a mission with Him in His world."[1] What mission do you think God has called you to at this time in your life?

Prayer

_____

_____

_____

_____

_____

_____

_____

11. Read each of these verses and write down what each teaches you about hope.

Romans 15:4 *Learn scriptures that gives us patience and comfort and His hope with in us*

1 Peter 1:3 *Jesus death - believing for Me — that I am his and he is always with me - guiding and giving hope for me and others*

Psalm 146:5 *Happiness and a Peace for all help in every circumstances - he was with me - I give you my Love, Peace, Hope and Trust.*

Romans 5:2-5 *His grace in tribulations helped to endure what was ahead - developing character - which gave me hope in my heart of His almighty love for me. (Faith and trust to always be there)*

---

1. Henry Blackaby, *Created to Be God's Friend: How God shapes Those He Loves* (Nashville: Thomas Nelson, 1999), 70–71.

GROUP DISCUSSION QUESTIONS

1. With a partner, discuss one thing you have been thinking about God this week or one thing that has distracted you from Him.

Scott needs work 6 - no income.

2. In what specific area or circumstance in your life today are you holding on to hope? What exactly have you been hoping for?

Boys - Craig continuing commitment to AA - God - Boys
Scott a permanet job College Ryan

3. Did anything you read in the chapter or heard on the DVD encourage you to hope? If so, what?

Watching TV - depressed -
Reading Daily Bread + Bible
lifts me up Spiritually

4. Lamentations is a poem written in response to a tragedy — the poet's home-
land was invaded, his city destroyed, his friends reduced to starvation and
captivity. Read Lamentations 3:16-26. What in this passage stands out to you?

_____

_____

_____

_____

_____

_____

_____

5. In what ways, if any, can you relate to the poet's grief?

_____

_____

_____

_____

_____

_____

_____

6. What do you think the poet means when he says, "The LORD is my portion"
(verse 24)? How do you make God your "portion"?

_____

_____

_____

_____

_____

_____

_____

_____

7. How can we call God faithful if He allows tragedy in our lives?

_____

_____

_____

_____

_____

_____

_____

8. How do you think you can have hope in God alone rather than put your hope in a desired outcome of your circumstances?

_____

_____

_____

_____

_____

_____

9. Read Romans 5:1-5. Paul says we have "the hope of the glory of God" (verse 2). What do you think this means?

_____

_____

_____

_____

_____

_____

10. Paul also says that hope doesn't disappoint us because God is pouring out His love to us through the Holy Spirit (see verse 5). In what ways, if any, are you experiencing that outpouring of love through the Spirit?

_____

_____

_____

_____

_____

11. Read aloud Psalm 62:5-7. Use this as a springboard to praise God and pray for each other.

_____

_____

_____

_____

_____

chapter six

BUT WHERE IS THE LAMB?

The Power of Faith

The kind of faith God values seems to develop best when everything fuzzes over, when God stays silent, when the fog rolls in.

—PHILIP YANCEY

ON MY OWN: INDIVIDUAL REFLECTION

I. Consider a time when God didn't answer your faith-filled prayers with the obvious "rescuing" intervention you had asked Him for. How did you feel? What specific questions about God, faith, life, and yourself were you left with?

_____

_____

_____

_____

_____

_____

_____

_____

_____

_____

2. Carol wondered if when the resolution of her Isaac experience wasn't favorable if it would be her fault for not having enough faith. Have you ever wondered this or struggled with this thought? Write about it here.

_____

_____

_____

_____

_____

3. What have you learned this week that has been helpful in your ongoing experience of processing what you've considered to be an "unhappy ending"?

_____

_____

_____

_____

4. In what area or circumstance do you currently find yourself asking God, "But where is the lamb?" Consider at least three specific needs you have that are not yet being met in obvious ways. List them as questions to God, such as, "Lord, why did my spouse betray me?" or "Why did my friend die of cancer?" or "Where is the money for the house payment?"

My Questions

1. _____

_____

_____

2. _____

_____

_____

3. _____

_____

_____

5. Hebrews 11:1 says, "Faith is confidence of what we hope for and assurance about what we do not see." In each of the three questions you listed, what are the unseen truths you are holding on to by faith? For example, you might be holding on to the seemingly "unseen" truth that God hasn't abandoned you. Write out what you believe by faith for each question.

Unseen Truths

1. _____
   _____

2. _____
   _____

3. _____
   _____
   _____

6. Reflect on these words from Jim Cymbala: "People with faith develop a second kind of sight. They see more than just the circumstances; they see God right beside them."[2] As you look at your current unresolved circumstances, where do you see God in proximity to you? Do you sense His right-beside-you presence? Or is He distant from you or even absent altogether? Describe exactly how your relationship with God looks and feels right now.

_____
_____
_____
_____
_____
_____
_____
_____

2. Jim Cymbala, with Dean Merrill, *Fresh Faith: What Happens When Real Faith Ignites God's People* (Grand Rapids, MI: Zondervan, 1999), 11.

7. Do you think that faith is more powerful when the lamb appears in the thicket for us, or can faith be even greater when the desired outcome doesn't happen? Describe your experience.

_____

_____

_____

_____

_____

_____

_____

8. Hebrews 11:39-40 talks of how the great heroes of the faith never received what had been promised:

> Not one of these people, even though their lives of faith were exemplary, got their hands on what was promised. God had a better plan for us: that their faith and our faith would come together to make one completed whole, their lives of faith not complete apart from ours. (MSG)

How does this passage comfort you?

_____

_____

_____

_____

_____

_____

9. Read Hebrews 11. Consider other people's faith that inspires or challenges you in your current Isaac experience — people such as Abraham, the heroes of

the faith, or people you know personally. In what specific ways do they inspire you to see your faith change and grow?

_____
_____
_____
_____
_____
_____
_____
_____

10. "Abraham looked up and there in a thicket he saw a ram caught by its horns" (Genesis 22:13). God did provide a sacrifice and provision for Abraham, symbolic of how God has provided our necessary sacrifice: Jesus. In Jesus, God has provided for all our ultimate needs, such as salvation, love, and comfort. How does the knowledge that God has provided the ultimate "ram in the thicket" change your perspective on your current Isaac experience?

_____
_____
_____
_____
_____
_____
_____
_____

11. Do a word search in the Bible on "faith." In the following chart, make a list of the verses that inspire you and write what each one means to you.

FAITH VERSE	WHAT THIS VERSE MEANS TO ME

GROUP DISCUSSION QUESTIONS

1. With one or two partners, discuss one thing you have been thinking about God this week or one thing that has distracted you from Him.

Scott - count Sue

I Peter 5:7,9 "Let him have all your worries and cares, for he is always thinking about you and watching everything that concerns you.

Be careful - watch out for attacks from Satan, your great enemy = Stand firm

2. Consider a time when God didn't answer your prayers with the "rescuing" intervention you asked for. How did you feel? What specific questions about God, faith, life, and yourself were you left with?

Bounced - Question my most motive for prayers - His Attitude Fairness - Satan jumping in - Forgiveness - God treats equally (loves)

3. What, if anything, did you learn this week that has helped you process what you've considered to be an "unhappy ending" in some situation? *MARK 12:30 Love God.*

Not doubting God - happy for His decision - because I know it is best for both. Happy about negative - I'll get over it but more anger with Scott & His feelings to God - other ways

Love God - Heart Soul Mind + Strength

4. Read Genesis 22:6-8. In what circumstance do you currently find yourself asking God, "Where is the lamb for the burnt offering?" What specific needs do you have that are not yet being met in ways known to you?

5. In your current unresolved circumstances, where do you see God in relation to you? Do you sense Him right beside you? Distant from you? Absent altogether?

_____

_____

_____

6. Do you think faith is more powerful when the lamb appears or when the desired outcome doesn't happen? Why?

_____

_____

_____

_____

7. Read Daniel 3:8-23. In painful circumstances in your own life, are you able to respond as the three men did in verses 16-17?

_____

_____

_____

_____

_____

8. Are you able to respond as these three men did in verse 18? Explain where you are in your process and how you would like to see your faith change and grow.

_____

_____

_____

_____

_____

9. Read Genesis 22:12-14. God provided Abraham with a ram in the thicket, just as He has ultimately provided our ram in the thicket, Jesus. How does knowing that God has provided for all your ultimate needs for salvation through Jesus impact your view of current circumstances?

_____

_____

_____

_____

_____

10. How can the group pray for you today?

_____

_____

_____

_____

_____

chapter seven

*E*MBRACING THE UPSIDE-DOWN NATURE OF THE CROSS

The Power of Joy

> *In the midst of the sorrows is consolation, in the midst of the darkness is light, in the midst of the despair is the hope, in the midst of Babylon is a glimpse of Jerusalem, and in the midst of the army of demons is the consoling angel.*
>
> —HENRI NOUWEN

ON *M*Y OWN: INDIVIDUAL REFLECTION

1. How often would you say you experience joy?

_____

never   rarely   occasionally   (often)   regularly

2. Has your joy through the years been more "celebratory" or "abiding"?

mixture _____ *continues for long term*

_____

_____

_____

_____

3. On a scale from 0 to 10, where would you say you are right now in terms of experiencing joy?

0	5	7-8	10
no joy	some joy		overflowing with joy

4. What do you find yourself thinking about as you answer these questions? Where are you placing your focus?

4 Funeral in 10 days.
Quiet time
Thankful for so many answered Prayers
So many highs — lows
I'm level.

5. Read and meditate on the full account of Jesus' last hours on earth in Matthew *wow* 26:17–28:20. What, specifically, do you notice in this account of Jesus' personal anguish, death, and resurrection that has the potential to unleash joy in the midst of your circumstances?

Very human — But the treat as Song Isl

6. Do you feel as though you're living closer to "Good Friday" or "Easter Sunday"? Explain.

7. "[Let us fix] our eyes on Jesus, the pioneer and perfecter of faith. For the joy set before him he endured the cross, scorning its shame, and sat down at the right hand of the throne of God" (Hebrews 12:2). How do the joy and hope of Jesus Christ and our future with Him allow you to endure your Isaac experiences?

Protector of Faith -
Joy of Everlasting time with Jesus because He died for Me -
Trusted - Sits next to the father God

8. Carol says, "The key to understanding authentic joy is in knowing that which gives rise to what the emotion is centered on." How can you take practical steps to do this, "fixing your eyes on Jesus," as the author of Hebrews says?

Wait - Watch - Read Bible - Pray

9. Do you know someone who is currently experiencing intense grief or heartache? If so, consider something concrete you can do to give that individual or family a taste of your love and God's comfort.

Wait - show you care.
Listen - to angry
Point Positive Things
Hold Jesus up as Our Hope
Endurance don't come easy sometimes
Faith - it is God's Will
Trust   "   "Be Done over Mine
Acceptance

10. Dr. Larry Crabb says, "Our shattered dreams are never random. They are always a piece in a larger puzzle, a chapter in a larger story. Pain is a tragedy. But it's never only a tragedy. . . . The journey to joy takes us through shattered dreams."[3] *Yes*

How do you respond to this? Has this been your experience, or does the whole idea make you angry? *Sometimes* Frightened? *Yes* Sad? *Yes* Write out a gut-level-honest prayer to God, telling Him exactly how you feel about the suffering He allows you and those you love to experience. Write until you have nothing more to say, and notice if you experience any shifts of energy or perspective as you pour out your heart to God on paper.

_____
_____
_____
_____
_____
_____
_____
_____
_____
_____
_____
_____
_____
_____
_____
_____
_____
_____

3. Larry Crabb, *Shattered Dreams* (Colorado Springs, CO: WaterBrook, 2001), 4, 198.

11. Read the following Bible passages:

> He will cover you with his feathers, and under his wings you will find refuge; his faithfulness will be your shield and rampart. (Psalm 91:4)

Bird wings tip   Buckler - Shield

> Weeping may stay for the night, but rejoicing comes in the morning. (Psalm 30:5)

> We do not want you to be uninformed about those who sleep in death, so that you do not grieve like the rest of mankind, who have no hope. (1 Thessalonians 4:13) We grieve but have Hope.

> We do not lose heart. Though outwardly we are wasting away, yet inwardly we are being renewed day by day. For our light and momentary troubles are achieving for us an eternal glory that far outweighs them all. So we fix our eyes not on what is seen, but on what is unseen, since what is seen is temporary, but what is unseen is eternal. (2 Corinthians 4:16-18)

Which one means the most to you right now? Why?

_____

_____

_____

_____

_____

_____

_____

_____

On an index card, write out the passage that means the most to you. Meditate on it and memorize it in the week ahead, asking God to use His Word to infuse you with supernatural and abiding joy.

GROUP DISCUSSION QUESTIONS

1. With a partner, discuss one thing you have been thinking about God this week or one thing that has distracted you from Him.

Dull - Numb

_____

_____

_____

_____

2. Have each person tell the group what his or her "history" with joy has been. Is it something you regularly, sometimes, or never experience? Does it come and go, based on circumstances, or does it stay around as a general sense of well-being?

_____

_____

_____

_____

_____

3. Where are you right now on the spectrum of joy? Are you experiencing abiding joy, or do you feel as if you are in the darkness of Good Friday?

Trust

_____

_____

_____

_____

_____

4. Read Hebrews 12:2-3:

> [Let us fix] our eyes on Jesus, the pioneer and perfecter of faith. For the joy set before him he endured the cross, scorning its shame, and sat down at the right hand of the throne of God. Consider him who endured such opposition from sinners, so that you will not grow weary and lose heart.

What was the joy that Jesus was looking forward to? Try to sketch as vivid a picture as possible.

Do Gods will for all who puts there trust faith & love in Heaven Father

5. Describe the joy that is ahead for you. How does this help you weather your current experiences?

Eternal life with Jesus. Need of more prayers for others.

6. Read 2 Corinthians 4:16-18:

> We do not lose heart. Though outwardly we are wasting away, yet inwardly we are being renewed day by day. For our light and momentary troubles are achieving for us an eternal glory that far outweighs

them all. So we fix our eyes not on what is seen, but on what is unseen, since what is seen is temporary, but what is unseen is eternal.

Explain in your own words why Paul didn't lose heart.

Forgiveness of Sin - Completely Forgiven
White as Snow -
Paul had his eye on Eternity

7. Do your troubles seem "light and momentary" (verse 17)? How do you think your perspective would change if you began to focus on the "unseen" and "eternal"?

Satan does His # personally (impatient
Keep my focus on His Word
answered Prayer - Trust
Faith I will Love Him -
kindness, caring etc. daily for Him

8. How can a person fix his eyes on what is unseen? What does that involve on a practical level?

No Pain - of Betrayal - Fun - Happiness -
Joy - loving everyone. Being Perfect
in Body Soul & Mind.

9. Which, if any, of the following thoughts give you joy? Talk about why they do or don't and what your experience with them has been.

- My suffering is making me a more loving and courageous person.

- My suffering is drawing others to Christ.
- Nothing can happen to me that can harm me in an ultimate way.
- Ultimately, I am going to be with Christ, where He will wipe away every tear.

_____

_____

_____

_____

_____

10. How can the group pray for you today?

_____

_____

_____

_____

_____

Donna – lever
Nancy –
Jim Hartsfield, John Brook

Donna is coming home Mar 4th
Thanks for your prayers.

chapter eight

FINDING OUR PURPOSE IN GOD'S GRAND STORY

The Power of Speaking Up

*To live by grace means to acknowledge my whole life story, the light side
and the dark. In admitting my shadow side I learn who I am and what
God's grace means.*

—BRENNAN MANNING

ON MY OWN: INDIVIDUAL REFLECTION

1. Carol says that ultimately "we win. Jesus wins. . . . We may not 'win' in the way
some people would measure a win. But we still win." Are you at the point now
where you can honestly join Carol in saying, "I win"? Write about where you are
in your journey.

_I count everyday a joy. Ok I reality
ups and downs. But when I think of my
walk with Christ. No Words but Praise
you Lord for loving me. & For hearing my
cries - know what is best for me and
those I pray for._
You are my awesome Lord.

2. Write a list of the victories — small and large — that you are already experiencing as you journey through your Isaac experience. (Depending on where you are in your journey, your victories might be things like finding the strength to do basic life tasks, such as getting out of bed in the morning.)

My Victories

Saving me as a child   *Walking me through hard*
Placing Positive in my life   *Blessing me with a be*
Loving my Husband #1   *Saving my Son — AAA*
Sons — Larry Todd   *(Know Satin is going to be ji*
Brought me back to the Lord   *Craig has boys & job.*
Saving my a second X-gun
Saving me from fatal car wreck
Health my mind & Spirit

3. Do you think that right now you are living as a victor? [*Yes*] In what specific ways can you begin to act on the fact that in God's grand story, "we win"?

Praying and being positive as to my day to day
walk with God. Some tearful times — but
count them joyful, because on my knees
talking to God — Pouring my soul out — Feeling
Him talk to me. Life How Precious — Life Is
Winning over the demons He casted out
I am a Winner! My Savior My Lord

[*No doubt*] 4. Currently do you think your experiences are causing you to run *from* God or to run *to* God? Rate this on a scale of 0 to 10, with 0 being "Running as fast as I can away from God," 3 being "My back is turned, and I am taking steady steps away," 5 being "I'm standing in the middle, not sure which way to turn," 7 being "I'm taking slow, tentative steps toward God," and 10 being "I'm running into His arms daily." *Satan at times makes things happen to cause doubt. But on my knees I ALWAYS SAVE MENTALLY.*

| 0 | 3 | 5 | 7 | 10 |

5. Everyone who is living with the heartache of an Isaac experience must make a choice every day — a choice between paralyzing despair and energizing faith. How can you make this a conscious decision every day? What specific choices do you need to make today and in the week ahead?

Count a joy to pray for others. Watching their lifes change. Even with losses they show positiveness loving the Lord. Watching them NOT turning away - but there cures in life is curved back towards Him.

6. In what ways have you needed to adjust to "a new kind of normal" as a result of your heart sacrifice? What physical, emotional, mental, and spiritual changes have you made?

New Friendship
Getting over losses
Making Changes -
No Smoking
No Medications
Staying Busy - Working Hard
Joy of ability to work.
Learning to Live on Less.
Not Needing Things
Loving Just Being Happy

7. Carol started to experience unexpected blessings due to her situation, such as spending more time playing games with her family and a simple smile from another woman in the prison visitation line. Write out a blessings list. Reflect and write for at least five minutes, refusing to think about any sorrows or frustrations but focusing on the positive things you've seen during your Isaac experience.

My Blessings

Many times lately I've been told you have a smile — That people say "they can tell I'm happy". I hear " Thank you Jesus for letting them see You in me."

Loving others — Not hiding but wanting to be around others.

But Pray " Listen — let me hear their stories Now."

8. "On the inside, where God is making new life, not a day goes by without his unfolding grace" (2 Corinthians 4:16, MSG). In the midst of a passage on troubles, Paul said that God is making new life. How are you experiencing new life? How are you experiencing His "unfolding grace"?

GRACE Unmerited help given to people by God —
Not feeling so sinful of past.
Living and wanting to change but not beating myself up if I make a mistake.
Remember to ask forgiveness — Not just excusing self or saying sorry.

ICor "So We do not lose heart. Though our outer self is wasting away, Our inner self is being renewed day by day.

9. Consider a time when you have been on the receiving end of the power of a shared story — a friend who openly and honestly told you about his or her past Isaac experience and how it gave you strength. Record the benefits of this experience.

I loved Barb's — reply and understanding so much I left out of a story that was so touching to me. But what she heard was not all of the story (Short version) not good But lovingly explained — Belly laugh joy — " I need to stop and listen to what I'm saying. Thanks that she so caring. Margo — brought such peace in soul!

8. Open your mouth for the mute, for the rights of all who are destitute

9 Open your mouth, judge righteously, defend the rights of the poor and needy.

10. How do you think God might be able to use your current story in His grander story? Do you feel that you are being called in any way to "speak up for the people who have no voice, for the rights of all the down-and-outers. Speak out for justice! Stand up for the poor and destitute!" (Proverbs 31:8-9, MSG)? If so, how?

I've questioned this, I'm not ashamed anymore. Others suffered the same and worse. Finding out WHY's feeling sorry for them. As abomination — and perverted people. But God Has given PEACE to my SOUL! JOY to my Life. FORGIVENESS from Others. Love has replaced it. From others and seeing Beauty all around that God has created —

Beauty in one day began with Him NO FEAR!

11. Jesus said to His disciples, "Right now I am storm-tossed. And what am I going to say? 'Father, get me out of this'? No, this is why I came in the first place. I'll say, 'Father, put your glory on display'" (John 12:27-28, MSG).

   Can you agree with Jesus' spirit of accepting the path of pain to bring God glory? Write out your prayer to God, and if you are ready, ask Him to use your story to put His glory on display.

John 12:27

Now is my soul troubled. And what shall I say: "Father, save me from this hour? But for this purpose I have come to this hour. 28. Father, glorify your name." Then a voice came from Heaven: "I HAVE glorified it, AND I will glorify it AGAIN."

30 The voice has come for your sake, not mine —

Let me only show you Praise Father. Your goodness to me and for me — because your Son suffered for me. My Son's and generations — may they all (my family) come to know Jesus and serve God after my days of generation till the end of time.

_____

_____

_____

_____

_____

_____

_____

_____

GROUP DISCUSSION QUESTIONS

1. Because it's the last week of the study, tell each other what you are grateful for about the group. How have the others in this group blessed you? What will you take away from this group?

_____

_____

_____

_____

_____

_____

2. Carol says, "Instead of running *from* God in the middle of our suffering, we are running *to* God." On a scale of 0 to 10, how true is this for you right now?

_____

_____

_____

_____

_____

_____

3. Read 2 Corinthians 12:7-10. Paul said that God gave him this thorn to keep him from being conceited. Based on how your character has been changing, why do you think God has given you a "thorn"?

_____

_____

_____

_____

_____

_____

_____

4. Why do you think God especially shows His strength amid our weakness?

_____

_____

_____

_____

_____

_____

_____

5. Think about God saying to you, "My grace is sufficient for you, for my power is made perfect in weakness" (verse 9). How do you respond emotionally to that verse? Is it a comfort, or is it unsettling?

_____

_____

_____

_____

_____

_____

_____

6. Do you think that right now you are acting like a victor — like someone who knows he or she will win in the end? In what specific ways can you act on the fact that in God's grand story, we win?

Winning is always humbling self-knowing I can NOT do good with out Him. His Spirit has always drawn me back to Him. No life circumstances - in mind - in my spirit (when I'm at my lowest - His Spirit picks me up). Less doubting more flexible to see a larger Picture - acceptance.

7. In an Isaac experience, each day one makes the choice to either choose God or remain paralyzed. What specific choices do you need to make today and in the week ahead that will enable you to go on living a productive and joyful life?

Consider it pure joy - whenever I'm faced (or Sons) with trials of any kind - because you know the testing of our faith produces perserverance. So I may MATURE and complete the task God has needed me to do - and lead me to his Glory.

JAMES 1:2-4

8. What victories and blessings — small and large — can you envision or are you already experiencing as you live through your Isaac experience?

Not doubting my mental state. Loving Life - just a plane day is Great. Feeling contented with what I have.

Concerns for our Children & Grand Children

9. In what ways have you needed to adjust to "a new kind of normal" as a result of your heart sacrifice? How do you feel about that?

Older - Health Financial - death

Appreciating the simplicity of life - don't have to impress anyone - or think less of self. Concerns for Others - Priviledge to Pray for them - Learned from all of Life. Good and Bad

10. Carol found purpose in her suffering: to speak up for prisoners' families who have no voice. What fruitful purpose might be in your suffering now or down the road?

It is my attitude that will help my (our) children to know Christ, or desires Him. That is why he spared me. My attitude and trust through words (even when they don't want to hear it) Praying for others outside my circle.

11. How can the group pray for you as you set out on your journey with God to live out your story for Him?

Finding my place to work more of a one on one - But guard my person circumstance to see the need of others now.

About the Author

CAROL KENT is a popular international public speaker who is best known for being dynamic, humorous, encouraging, and biblical. She is a former radio-show cohost and has been a guest many times on *Focus on the Family* and a featured speaker at Women of Faith and Women of Joy arena events. She has also spoken at The Praise Gathering for Believers and at Vision New England's Congress and is a frequent speaker at Extraordinary Women events.

Carol has spoken internationally in South Africa, Germany, China, Korea, Hong Kong, Guatemala, Mexico, and Canada. She regularly appears on a wide variety of nationally syndicated radio and television broadcasts. Past appearances have included *Dateline NBC*, *CNN Live*, *The Billy Graham Television Special*, "*It Is Written*" *TV*, *Family Talk*, *On Main Street*, *LIFE Today with James Robison*, *Prime Time America*, *Midday Connection*, *Family Life Today*, and *100 Huntley Street*. Carol has also been a keynote speaker for the televised and nationally syndicated women's conference sponsored by Church Communications Network.

She is the president of Speak Up Speaker Services, a Christian speakers' bureau, and the founder and director of the Speak Up Conference, where she equips the next generation to speak, write, and lead. She founded the nonprofit organization Speak Up for Hope, which benefits the families of incarcerated individuals.

Carol holds a master's degree in communication arts and a bachelor's degree in speech education. She has taught speech and drama, and she has directed women's ministries at a large midwestern church. She is a member of the

Advanced Writers and Speakers Association and serves on the advisory board of MOPS International.

Her books include *Between a Rock and a Grace Place*, *A New Kind of Normal*, *Miracle on Hope Hill* (cowritten with Jennie Afman Dimkoff), *When I Lay My Isaac Down*, *Becoming a Woman of Influence*, *Mothers Have Angel Wings*, *Secret Longings of the Heart*, *Tame Your Fears*, *Speak Up with Confidence*, and *Detours, Tow Trucks, and Angels in Disguise*. She also cowrote with Karen Lee-Thorp the DESIGNED FOR INFLUENCE Bible studies. Carol has been featured on the cover of *Today's Christian Woman*, and her articles have been published in a wide variety of magazines.

To schedule Carol to speak for your event, please contact:

Speak Up Speaker Services
586.481.7661
www.SpeakUpSpeakerServices.com
or
www.CarolKent.org

E-mail: Speakupinc@aol.com

For information on the Speak Up Conference,
go to SpeakUpConference.com.

For information on the ministry to inmates and their families,
go to SpeakUpforHope.org.

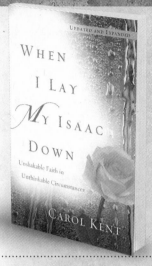
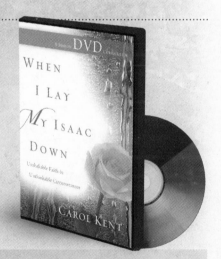